100X MINDSET

14 RULES FOR UNSTOPPABLE GROWTH, WEALTH, AND DISCIPLINE

Mando CT

CONTENTS

INTRODUCTION

You Are Far More Powerful Than You've Been Told

At some point in your life, you were conditioned to settle.

You were told, sometimes subtly, sometimes directly, that life is supposed to be hard, that success is reserved for the lucky, that ambition is risky, and that you should be grateful for what you have, even if it leaves you unfulfilled. You were encouraged to follow the rules, do your best, stay safe, avoid failure, and never expect too much.

And so, you lowered your standards. You traded dreams for distractions. You began to accept less - less energy, less joy, less clarity, less purpose. Over time, you began to convince yourself that this was normal. That this was life.

But it isn't. Not even close.

My name is Mando CT, and I wrote this book to tell you the truth that no one told me when I was younger: **you are more powerful than you've been led to believe**. There is a version of you, already within you, that is stronger, clearer, wealthier, healthier, and more fulfilled than anything you've known so far. The only difference between who you are and who you could become is the mindset you are willing to adopt today.

Let me be very direct with you. I was not born into wealth. I didn't inherit opportunities. I grew up in Liverpool, England, in a working-class family. I've faced hardship, hunger, empty bank accounts, and moments of complete uncertainty. I've sat on buses to nowhere, going to jobs that drained my soul. I've experienced the hopelessness of seeing no way out until I created one.

Through years of trial, failure, and self-discipline, I built a life of freedom and purpose. I became financially independent. I built a business that now influences millions across the globe. I did it without a silver spoon, without shortcuts, and without compromising my values. And if I could do it, you could too.

That is what this book is about.

100X MINDSET is not another motivational book filled with clichés and empty promises. It is a practical, proven system for rewiring your thinking, rebuilding your identity, and multiplying your results personally, professionally, financially, and spiritually.

You will learn the mental frameworks I used to go from broke to abundant, confused to clear, and stuck to free. You will discover why discipline beats motivation, why clarity creates momentum, and why mindset is the root cause of every result you've ever had.

We will dismantle the lies you've been told about success. We will replace them with tested principles that you can apply immediately. You will gain tools to manage your time, your energy, your habits, and your focus. You will learn how to cultivate emotional strength, financial intelligence, and the confidence to pursue what truly matters to you.

You may not have control over where you started. But you have full control over where you go from here.

There is no more powerful force in the world than a human being who decides to live intentionally. This book is your invitation to become that person.

It won't be easy. It will require sacrifice, honesty, courage and consistent action. But it will change everything.

Now is the time to let go of the story that has held you back. Now is the time to replace self-doubt with self-leadership.

Now is the time to raise your standards and become the person your future is waiting for.

Welcome to *100X MINDSET*.

Let's begin.

- Mando CT

CHAPTER 1: LIVE WITH INTEGRITY

The First Rule of a 100X Life

If you were to study every truly successful person, those who have achieved not only wealth but also peace of mind, fulfilling relationships, and a meaningful life, you would find one principle that stands at the foundation of it all: **integrity**.

Integrity is the highest form of human excellence. It is the habit of being honest with yourself and with others. It is the decision to do what is right, even when it is inconvenient, uncomfortable, or unseen. It is the single most important habit you can build if you wish to live a life of purpose and power.

Without integrity, nothing else lasts.

For years, I chased the version of success the world promotes: popularity, applause, money in the account, and luxury on display. I believed that these visible signs meant I was on the right track. And in some ways, I was. I had built a global following. I had travelled the world. I had earned more than I ever imagined possible as a boy growing up in Liverpool.

But somewhere along the way, I began to feel something shift. I was achieving more but feeling less. My schedule was full, but my soul was empty. I realised that I had built a lifestyle but not a life. And I had done it by compromising my own sense of alignment. I had become so busy building an image that I had neglected the truth of who I wanted to be.

That moment of clarity was not comfortable. But, it was necessary because it brought me back to the one principle that has never failed me: integrity.

I made the decision to rebuild everything from the inside out. And that decision changed everything.

The most important relationship you have is the one you have with yourself. Every time you keep a promise to yourself, no matter how small, you reinforce that relationship. You tell yourself, "I can rely on me." That is the essence of self-confidence: not false bravado, but the quiet certainty that comes from honouring your own word.

When you commit to waking up early, and you do, it builds trust. When you promise yourself to eat well and follow through, it builds strength. When you admit a mistake, instead of hiding it, it builds character.

Without integrity, your self-image erodes. You may appear confident on the outside, but inside, you know you cannot count on yourself. And that internal conflict will eventually sabotage everything you build.

Integrity is how you align your words, your thoughts, and your actions. And when all three are in agreement, you gain power.

Integrity affects everything: your reputation, your relationships, your income, your health, and your ability to sleep at night.

In business, integrity leads to trust, and trust is the foundation of every lasting success. Clients return to people they trust. Teams follow leaders they believe in. Money flows towards reliability, not talent alone.

In your personal life, integrity builds depth in your relationships. People open up to those who are grounded. Family bonds strengthen when they are built on honesty. Friendships deepen when people know your values are not for sale.

And in your own mind, integrity gives you peace. When you know you are living truthfully, you are not carrying the burden of pretending. You are free to focus, to create, to lead. Your conscience becomes your compass. And peace becomes your power.

Making the Commitment

You do not need to be perfect to live with integrity. You only need to be consistent. That means telling the truth, even when it is difficult. It means owning your mistakes without shifting blame. It means setting standards and holding yourself to them. It is not an easy path. But it is the only one that leads to lasting fulfilment.

One of the great turning points in my life was the moment I decided I would rather succeed slowly with integrity than quickly with compromise. I would rather be respected for who I am than admired for who I pretend to be. Make that same decision today.

Let your life speak for itself. Let your actions match your words. Let the values you hold internally be reflected externally. The more you align, the more you accelerate. Integrity is not just a moral concept. It is a success multiplier.

When you live with integrity, you move through life with clarity, with focus, and with strength. And that is the foundation of a 100X mindset.

Action Steps: Living With Integrity

1. Define Your Non-Negotiables

Take 10 minutes to write down your top five personal values and principles that you refuse to compromise. These could include honesty, reliability, health, discipline, or faith. These values will form the basis of your personal code.

1.   4.

2.   5.

3.

2. Identify Where You Are Out of Alignment

Review the key areas of your life: health, relationships, work, money, and habits. Ask yourself, *"Where am I saying one thing but doing another?"* Write down at least three areas where your actions do not match your stated values.

3. Make One Promise You Will Keep

Choose one small, meaningful action you can commit to this week that reflects your integrity. It could be as simple as waking up on time, completing a task you've been avoiding, or having an honest conversation. Keep that promise, no matter what.

4. Practice Daily Honesty With Yourself

At the end of each day, reflect for five minutes and ask yourself, *"Did I live in alignment with my values today?"* If not, do not judge, adjust. Integrity grows through awareness and correction, not perfection.

5. Communicate With Clarity and Accountability

In your next difficult conversation, whether personal or professional, commit to being clear, honest, and respectful. Speak the truth with courage and kindness. Integrity in communication builds unshakeable trust.

6. Audit Your Commitments

Go through your calendar and your task list. Are there things you've committed to out of guilt, fear, or pressure? If so, either recommit fully or respectfully decline. Half-hearted commitments weaken your integrity and dilute your focus.

7. Create Your Integrity Standard Statement

Write a one-sentence personal standard you will live by, something you can repeat each morning. For example:

"I will live in such a way that I respect the man I see in the mirror."

Say it daily. Let it guide your decisions.

CHAPTER 2: DO WHAT IGNITES YOUR SOUL

The Second Rule of a 100X Life

One of the greatest misconceptions in life is the belief that achievement creates happiness. This is not only incorrect; it is dangerously misleading.

The truth is the exact opposite: **happiness precedes achievement**.

When you are energised, fulfilled, and emotionally connected to your work, you operate with clarity, creativity, and commitment. When you are drained, frustrated, or misaligned, even the smallest task becomes a burden. If you want to succeed, not temporarily, but sustainably, you must first discover what makes you come alive.

In other words, you must do what ignites your soul.

For example, from a young age, most of us were told a specific story: play it safe, get a steady job, choose security over passion, and never ask for too much. We were taught that life is a ladder, and the goal is simply to climb higher, whether we enjoy the climb or not. We were rewarded for conformity, not curiosity.

You cannot manufacture passion.
You cannot force yourself to care about something that doesn't speak to your spirit. You might comply, but you will never fully commit. You might survive, but you will never truly live.

The world is full of people climbing the wrong ladders. And many only realise it once they've reached the top.

My Breaking Point and Breakthrough

When I left Liverpool in 1997 to DJ in the Greek Islands, I didn't have a detailed plan. What I had was a fire inside me. I knew that if I stayed in my old life, I would be trading my potential for predictability. And something in me refused to die that slowly.

For four years, I played music under the stars, learned a new language, and built friendships across cultures. For the first time in my life, I was doing work that gave me energy, not just income. I was no longer a cog in someone else's machine; I was alive.

That experience became a turning point. It showed me that it is not only *possible* to align your work with your soul; it is necessary if you want to sustain long-term success and joy.

There is a noticeable difference between people who are goal-driven and those who are purpose-driven. Goal-driven people are often externally motivated. They push themselves with deadlines, targets, and external rewards. And while that can produce short bursts of performance, it is rarely sustainable.

Purpose-driven people, on the other hand, are internally fuelled. They work not because they *have to* but because they *choose to*. They are connected to a cause greater than themselves. Their work is an extension of their identity, not a rejection of it.

This is why you will often see purpose-driven people outperform others in the long run. They are not pushing; they are pulled. They are not grinding; they are flowing. They are not chasing success; they are becoming it.

The 100X Mindset is not about working harder than everyone else. It is about working in alignment with who you really are.

Many people stay in careers, businesses, and relationships that drain them because they are afraid of change. They believe that security is worth the cost of fulfilment.

They convince themselves that playing it safe is noble and that desire is dangerous.

But let me ask you directly: **What is the greater risk, failing at something you love or succeeding at something you hate?**

I have taken many risks in my life. I have walked away from a safe income, from approval, from comfort. But I have never once regretted following what made me feel alive.

When you follow what ignites your soul, you will face fear. You will face failure. But you will also face **yourself**. And in that moment, you will realise that the worst kind of failure is to never try.

When your work and your values are aligned, your performance multiplies. You no longer waste energy pretending. You no longer compromise your spirit to earn a living. You show up fully. You speak with conviction. You produce from a place of power, not pressure.

And others will notice.

Energy is contagious. When you are doing what you were born to do, people will be drawn to you. Opportunities will find you. The right clients, the right partnerships, the right breakthroughs, they all respond to authenticity.

You will stop chasing success. You will start attracting it.

You were not designed for mediocrity. You were not created to survive your own life. There is something inside you that burns. Something that pulls you forward. Do not ignore it.

If you want to live with the 100X Mindset, you must build your life around what energises you. Not because it's easy, but because it's *real*. And real success only exists in alignment.

Action Steps: Living What Ignites You

1. Identify What Energises You

Reflect on moments where you felt most alive, engaged, and at peace. What were you doing? Who were you with? Write down three recurring patterns.

2. Evaluate Your Current Work

Ask yourself: *"Does my current work reflect my core strengths and values?"* Be honest. Rate it from 1 to 10 in terms of fulfilment.

3. Design Your Alignment Plan

Choose one small change you can make this week to bring more passion into your work. It may be a new habit, a new project, or a new conversation.

4. Create a Personal Mission Statement

In one sentence, define what you stand for and what kind of work you want your life to express. Read it every morning.

5. Risk Forward

Take one brave action this week towards something that excites you, even if you feel uncertain. Action creates clarity.

CHAPTER 3: SURROUND YOURSELF WITH GREATNESS

The Third Rule of a 100X Life

Your Environment Determines Your Altitude

You become the average of the five people you spend the most time with.

Your thinking, your habits, your income, your health, and your emotional state, are all directly influenced by the people you allow into your daily life. Whether you realise it or not, your environment is shaping you every day. The question is: Is it shaping you towards your potential, or is it moving you away from it?

If you want to develop the 100X Mindset, you must become ruthlessly intentional about who you allow to speak into your life, who you give your energy to, and who you choose to become like.

When I was younger, I didn't fully understand how powerful my environment was. I surrounded myself with people who were kind, loyal, and familiar, but they were not growing. They were not aiming higher. They were not thinking bigger. And slowly, without even realising it, I began to shrink my own vision to match theirs.

It was only when I stepped outside of that circle that I began meeting people who were playing life at a higher level, as a result of which, I experienced a shift. I saw what was possible. I saw how they thought, how they moved, how they acted. And I realised that greatness is never an accident. It is the result of exposure, discipline, and influence.

The right people will expand you. The wrong people will shrink you.

Many people wait for their environment to change. They hope that one day they'll "find" better people or that someone will discover them. That's not how success works. If you want to elevate your life, you must **create your environment**. You must choose who you learn from, who you listen to, and who you allow to speak into your vision.

This means making bold decisions. It means letting go of relationships that no longer reflect your values. It means seeking out mentors, coaches, and peers who are operating at the level you aspire to reach. It may even mean being uncomfortable for a season as you step into new rooms where you are no longer the smartest, strongest, or most experienced.

But that's where growth happens.

Every time I've levelled up in my life, it's because I changed who I was learning from. From my time in the Greek Islands as a DJ to my journey through investment banking to building a global platform in the crypto space, each breakthrough began by getting around people who were further ahead of me. I asked questions. I listened. I adapted. And I grew.

Mentors, Coaches, Allies, Your Success Ecosystem

One of the fastest ways to accelerate your progress is to study people who have already achieved what you desire. Success leaves clues. A good mentor can save you years of trial and error. A skilled coach can help you see your blind spots and hold you accountable to your standards. And a strong circle of allies can keep your energy high when challenges arise.

You do not need hundreds of people. You need the **right few.**

Start by identifying who inspires you. Who is already living the kind of life you want, spiritually, financially, and emotionally? Who challenges you to think bigger, act bolder, and rise higher? Follow them. Learn from them. Invest in their content, their books, their programmes. Reach out when you can. Model their discipline.

Do not make the mistake of trying to do everything alone. Even the strongest warriors need a tribe.

Your environment is more than people. It is also your space, your routine, your media, your habits. Everything you allow into your life is either pulling you forward or holding you back.

Take a close look at your daily surroundings. Does your physical space inspire clarity and focus? Do the conversations you're having encourage growth? Do the books, videos, and content you consume lift your thinking or distract it?

Designing your environment means taking responsibility for every element of your life and aligning it with your vision. It means eliminating distractions, avoiding gossip, and creating routines that support high performance. It means choosing to be in places, physically and mentally, where greatness is the standard.

If you want to rise, build a world around you that expects you to rise.

You are not simply a product of your ambition; you are a product of your associations. The people you allow into your mind and your life will either water your potential or poison it.

To live with the 100X Mindset, you must surround yourself with greatness. You must seek it, honour it, and protect it. Because the truth is, you will never outperform your environment for long. If you want to change your life, change your circle.

Action Steps: Upgrading Your Circle

1. Audit Your Five

Write down the five people you spend the most time with. Ask yourself: *Do these individuals reflect the future I want to create?* Be honest.

2. Identify Your Mentors

Choose three people, living or historical, whose lives inspire you. Begin studying them intensely. Read their books, watch their interviews, and take notes.

3. Create Your Growth Environment

Design a weekly space for personal growth. This could be a mastermind, a reading hour, or weekly coaching. Protect it on your calendar.

4. Limit Negative Influence

Reduce exposure to individuals who drain your energy, complain consistently, or mock ambition. You don't need to cut them out harshly; just rise so high they can no longer reach you.

5. Build Intentional Relationships

Reach out to one new person each month who inspires you: send a thoughtful message, offer value, and ask a question. Relationships are built, not found. You will rise as high as your environment allows. Choose wisely. Act intentionally. Surround yourself with greatness.

CHAPTER 4: GROW 1% EVERY DAY

The Fourth Rule of a 100X Life

The greatest advantage in life does not belong to the most intelligent, the most talented, or the most connected. It belongs to those who are willing to **grow deliberately, consistently, and incrementally** every single day.

Growth is not a moment. It's a method. It is not a sprint. It is a strategy. Those who understand this principle, what I call the *1% Rule*, hold a power that compounds over time, turning small beginnings into extraordinary outcomes.

If you apply this principle consistently, you will begin to outperform your previous self, outpace your former limitations, and outgrow the environment you once believed would contain you.

This is how I went from being broke in Liverpool to becoming financially free in Dubai.

Not through dramatic leaps. Not through luck. But by getting 1% better every day.

The Illusion of Motivation

Most people overestimate the power of motivation and underestimate the value of discipline. Motivation is emotional; it comes and goes. Discipline, in contrast, is a decision. It is what you do *regardless* of how you feel. And that is what builds greatness.

When I was living in Liverpool, trying to make sense of my life, there were many days when I had no motivation. I had more questions than answers. I didn't know how I would change my circumstances; I only knew I had to start.

So, I began with what I could control: my habits.

I started reading ten pages a day. I journaled what I learned. I began waking up earlier, eating cleaner, moving my body, and learning about wealth, not just how to earn it but how to think like someone who already had it.

None of these changes were impressive on their own. But over time, the **compound effect** began to take root. Small wins became patterns. Patterns became confidence. Confidence became momentum.

This is the principle you must embrace if you want to change your life.

Let's do the math. If you improve by just 1% each day, you don't grow by 365% in a year. You grow by **3,778%**. That is the power of compounding. Each gain builds upon the last. And the further you go, the faster you move.

But the opposite is also true. If you allow yourself to decline by just 1% per day through procrastination, distraction, and disorganisation, you will reduce your capacity to less than 3% of what it could have been.

Growth is not a neutral process. You are either growing or shrinking. You are either climbing or sliding. There is no such thing as standing still.

To grow by 1% every day, you must create a system. The key is to remove friction, automate excellence, and treat your daily routine as the most important asset you own.

Here is the core of the routine that changed my life:

1. Wake early with intention. Begin the day with clarity, not chaos. Don't reach for your phone; reach for focus.

2. Read to learn. Spend 15–30 minutes each morning reading something that stretches your thinking. Knowledge is leverage.

3. Journal with purpose. Record what you've learned, how you feel, and what you are focused on. Reflection cements growth.

4. Move your body. Even 20 minutes of physical activity primes your brain, increases your energy, and sharpens your focus.

5. Eliminate distractions. Turn off unnecessary notifications. Limit reactive behaviours. Focus on what moves your life forward.

6. Track your progress. What gets measured improves. Review your growth weekly. Adjust as needed, but always keep moving.

This system is not complicated. But it is powerful. And if you practise it daily, it will transform your life faster than you ever imagined.

People often see the headlines, 'Mando CT builds million-follower platform,' 'Crypto influencer turned entrepreneur,' 'Dubai villas and supercars,' but they don't see the early mornings, the skipped parties, the quiet discipline.

They don't see the hundreds of hours spent reading when no one was watching. They don't see the decision made to skip alcohol in favour of clarity. They don't see the years of 1% improvements that eventually turned into exponential outcomes.

There was no miracle moment. Just small wins, stacked daily.

And you can do the same.

The most important transformation you will make is internal. When you grow by 1% every day, your identity begins to shift. You no longer see yourself as someone who struggles; you begin to see yourself as someone who **improves**.

This shift creates integrity. It builds self-trust. And over time, it becomes your default way of living.

You no longer need to rely on bursts of energy. You've built something better: a *standard*.

You don't need to change your life in one day. You need to commit to changing **something** every day.

Success is not the result of a breakthrough moment; it is the result of many quiet mornings, unseen efforts, and private disciplines. The 100X Mindset is built through repetition, not revolution.

Improve by 1% today. And then do it again tomorrow. Let time and consistency take care of the rest.

Action Steps: Grow 1% Every Day

1. Design Your Morning Routine

Create a morning plan that includes reading, journaling, movement, and reflection. Keep it simple but consistent.

2. Choose One Growth Focus

Select one area of your life: health, finances, mindset, or relationships, and commit to improving it daily by 1%. Write down what this looks like.

3. Track Your 1%

At the end of each day, ask yourself: *"Where did I grow today?"* Record even the smallest win.

4. Replace One Weak Habit

Identify a behaviour that is holding you back. Replace it with a stronger alternative. For example, trade social media scrolling for 15 minutes of reading.

5. Stay the Course for 30 Days

Commit to the 1% rule for the next 30 days. Don't aim to be perfect. Aim to be consistent. Watch your identity evolve.

You are not here to remain who you were yesterday. You are here to expand. To evolve. To become the person your potential demands.

Grow 1% today.

CHAPTER 5: EMBRACE FAILURE AS YOUR TEACHER

The Fifth Rule of a 100X Life

Every Setback Holds a Lesson That Can Change Your Life

There is a truth that successful people understand deeply, one that separates them from those who give up when life becomes difficult. They understand that:

Failure is not the opposite of success. It is a requirement for it.

Failure, handled correctly, is not defeat; it's feedback. It is not a wall; it's a mirror. It shows you exactly where you need to grow, what you need to improve, and who you need to become to reach the next level.

The most successful individuals in any field are not those who avoided failure. They are those who embraced it, learned from it, and used it as fuel for greater achievement.

You can do the analysis yourself, look at the people you admire, no matter if they are celebrities, and notice that all of them have failed at some point in their careers: Michael Jordan, J.K. Rowling, Mark Zuckerberg...

If you are serious about adopting the 100X Mindset, you must make peace with failure. You must stop seeing it as a curse and start recognising it as a coach.

When you fail, and you will, you are receiving priceless data. You are learning what doesn't work. You are uncovering a weakness in your process, your strategy, or your thinking. And that is valuable.

The only true failure is the failure to reflect. The failure to adjust. The failure to try again with better insight.

Every setback offers one of two things: a reason to stop or a reason to grow. The choice is entirely yours.

In my own life, every major breakthrough was preceded by what, at the time, felt like a breakdown. I've experienced financial loss, broken trust, personal regret, and moments where I questioned whether I was truly meant for more.

But each time, after the emotion passed, I forced myself to ask the key question: *"What is this teaching me?"*

That question transformed pain into progress.

I still remember the moment I ran out of money in my early twenties. I was living in a flat that I could no longer afford; the rent was unpaid, the fridge was empty, and the phone was disconnected. I had tried to start a business, made the wrong partnerships, and ended up worse off than when I started. I felt like a failure.

But that experience taught me the value of financial awareness. It taught me to separate hype from substance. It forced me to learn about money, not just how to earn it, but how to manage it, multiply it, and protect it.

That lesson laid the groundwork for my later success in cryptocurrency and investment.

Another moment came when I realised I was surrounding myself with people who applauded my comfort but never challenged my growth. I had failed to audit my circle. That failure cost me time, energy, and years of potential. But it taught me the irreplaceable value of being around those who sharpen you.

Failure can either define you or refine you. The decision is yours.

What Successful People Do Differently

The difference between those who rise and those who remain stuck is not talent. It is not luck. It is not education.

It is how they interpret their setbacks.

Unsuccessful people take failure personally. They internalise it. They begin to believe that failure means *they* are a failure. They lose momentum. They lose confidence. They stop trying.

Successful people, on the other hand, view failure impersonally. They do not take it as a reflection of their worth but as a reflection of their current method. They do not collapse under the weight of disappointment. They adapt. They adjust. They apply what they've learned and keep moving.

In truth, successful people fail **more often** than unsuccessful people. The difference is that they don't stay down. They treat each fall as a step forward.

The Emotional Power of Resilience

Resilience is the emotional strength to keep moving forward when everything in you wants to stop. It is the refusal to allow a bad chapter to become a bad ending. And it is one of the defining traits of the 100X Mindset.

To become resilient, you must learn to regulate your emotions during adversity. It is easy to be positive when everything is going well. True strength is revealed in difficulty. It is built in silence. It is proven when no one is clapping for you.

You must become your own source of motivation. Your own anchor. Your own comeback story.

When I failed publicly, I had to go home and rebuild privately. When I lost money, I had to swallow my pride and start again. When I made mistakes, I had to confront them and grow. That is how resilience is forged, not through comfort but through courage.

Failure is not something to fear. It is something to study.

If you are willing to view every setback as feedback, every mistake as a message, and every fall as a test of your future strength, you will rise faster, grow deeper, and succeed further than those who fear failure ever will.

The 100X Mindset is not a mindset of perfection. It is a mindset of progression. And every step forward, even if it begins with a fall, is a step in the right direction.

Action Steps: Learning from Failure

1. Redefine Failure in Your Mind

Write this sentence and repeat it daily: *"Failure is feedback, not identity."*

2. Reflect on a Past Setback

Choose one failure from the past year. Write down everything it taught you. List what you would do differently now and how that failure served your growth.

3. Adopt a New Response Pattern

When the next challenge or mistake arises, practise this three-step response: Pause. Analyse. Adjust. Don't react emotionally; respond intentionally.

4. Share Your Lessons

Speak openly about a failure and what you learned from it with someone you trust. Vulnerability breeds strength, and ownership breeds credibility.

5. Commit to Resilience

Make a list of the three hardest things you've ever overcome. Use them as proof: *If I overcame that, I can overcome anything in the future.*

You are not here to be flawless. You are here to become *fearless.* Embrace failure as your greatest teacher. It is never there to break you. Only to build you.

CHAPTER 6: MASTER YOUR MORNING

The Sixth Rule of a 100X Life

How You Start Your Day Is How You Shape Your Life

There is one principle I discovered early in my personal transformation that has never failed me, no matter the circumstances or season of life. It is simple, but it is powerful beyond measure:

Your first hour determines your direction for the entire day.

This is not just a motivational statement. It's a neurological, emotional, and behavioural reality. What you do in the first 60 minutes after waking up sets the tone for your energy, your clarity, your productivity, and your state of mind. When you take command of your mornings, you take command of your life.

If you look closely at any high-performing individual, whether in business, athletics, the arts or leadership, you will find they don't stumble into their mornings. They structure them. They guard them. They treat them as sacred.

That is what I began doing when I decided to rebuild my life, not from crisis or chaos, but from conscious intention.

It changed everything.

There was a point, years ago, when I was in a financial drought. No petrol. No rent paid. No direction. I had followed distractions instead of purpose, and it had left me empty physically, emotionally, and spiritually. One morning, I sat alone on the edge of a borrowed bed in a flat I couldn't afford, staring at my reflection in a cracked mirror.

Something inside me snapped, not in defeat, but in decision.

I realised that if I could not change my environment overnight, I would change **how I entered it**. I would no longer begin my days with noise, with reaction, with aimlessness. I would wake with clarity. I would rise with gratitude. I would train my mind, my body, and my spirit as if my future depended on it, because it did.

That morning was not special. But what followed became extraordinary.

The 100X Morning Routine

My transformation began not with money but with **a morning**. Below is the exact structure I still follow today, a routine that allowed me to go from survival to success, from reactive to intentional, from broke to global.

1. Early Rising

I wake before the noise of the world can reach me. This time is mine. No distractions. No phones. Just clarity.

2. Gratitude and Prayer

Before any goal, I centre my mind on what already exists. I thank the universe, I speak to God, and I express gratitude, not for what I hope to gain, but for what I already have. Gratitude transforms pressure into power.

3. Movement

I engage in physical activity, sometimes a full workout, other times a brisk walk or stretching. Movement energises the brain, strengthens the body, and builds discipline before the first challenge appears.

4. Journaling

I write down what I'm thinking, what I'm focused on, and who I'm becoming. I record lessons, wins, and areas to grow. This reflection grounds me in the present and connects me to my vision.

5. Learning

I read. Even 10 pages of the right book can rewire your mindset for the entire day. I choose material that stretches me and raises my standards.

6. Visualisation and Intent Setting

I visualise my goals, not vaguely, but in vivid detail. I set intentions for the day and decide what outcome I am responsible for creating. I see it before I live it.

This routine takes between 60 and 90 minutes. It's not about perfection; it's about ownership. You may not be able to control everything in life, but you can control **how you begin**.

And how you begin determines how you continue.

What you repeatedly do becomes who you are. When you practise the same habits every morning, habits that are aligned with your values, you begin to rewire the subconscious mind. You build a new identity, one act at a time.

Your subconscious does not respond to what you *wish* for. It responds to what you *prove*. That is why mornings matter. They are not just about productivity. They are about programming. Each repetition tells your inner world: *this is who I am now.*

Over time, doubt fades. Clarity expands. Confidence strengthens.

And your results begin to match your new internal reality.

Tools for Tracking and Improving

Success without measurement is unsustainable. That's why I recommend using simple tools to track your morning performance. I use a daily log that tracks:

1. Wake-up time

2. Movement completed

3. Gratitude/Journaling

4. Learning minutes

5. Top three intentions for the day

6. End-of-day reflection

These six metrics allow me to stay accountable. When I slip, I can see it clearly. When I progress, I can feel it tangibly. You don't need complex systems. You need consistency. You need proof that your discipline is building momentum.

Your habits are your evidence. Let them speak. The morning is not the beginning of the day; it is the launchpad of your future.

When you master your morning, you stop chasing your life and start creating it. You gain emotional control, mental clarity, physical energy, and spiritual direction, all before the rest of the world has begun to react.

Do not let your mornings be dictated by your phone, your fears, or your circumstances. Rise with purpose. Own the hour. Rewrite your identity. This is the 100X Mindset in motion.

Action Steps: Mastering Your Morning

1. Commit to a Start Time

Choose your wake-up time and honour it every day this week. Even if it's just 30 minutes earlier, show yourself that you can lead yourself.

2. Build a Morning Power Hour

Create a simple, repeatable routine that includes gratitude, movement, reading, and journaling. Start small. Stay consistent.

3. Design Your Environment for Focus

Place your journal, workout gear, and reading material within reach. Make it easy to start the first hour.

4. Track Your Habits for 7 Days

Use a habit tracker to monitor your progress. Reflect each evening on how your morning affected the rest of your day.

5. Visualise Your Identity Daily

Spend five minutes each morning visualising the person you are becoming. Feel it emotionally. Affirm it clearly. Then live it.

CHAPTER 7: TAKE CONTROL OF YOUR HEALTH

The Seventh Rule of a 100X Life

I want to start rule number 7 by debunking an internal myth that 99% of people have: Your health is not about appearance. It is about performance. It is about your ability to sustain effort, to respond under pressure, and to remain focused when others fatigue. Energy is not optional; it is the invisible currency behind every productive hour, every strategic decision, and every successful outcome.

No matter how talented or intelligent you are, if you do not have physical vitality, your execution will suffer. If you are serious about building anything worthwhile – business, family, or legacy – you must **treat your body as your first enterprise.**

I learned this lesson through experience.

For years, I operated under the illusion that pushing myself harder would produce greater results. Long nights, skipped meals, and inconsistent sleep, I wore these like a badge of honour. But instead of gaining momentum, I noticed something else: diminished clarity, slower recovery, mood swings, and decision fatigue.

It became clear to me that **exhaustion is not a prerequisite for success. It is a penalty.**

Sustainable performance requires you to **manage your energy as seriously as you manage your money**. You do not overspend your finances without consequences. Why overspend your body?

So, I made the decision to correct the imbalance, not with complexity, but with structure. I began treating health as a daily investment. That shift changed my personal productivity, sharpened my thinking, and added depth to every role I played as an entrepreneur, father, husband, and strategist.

If you want to perform at a high level consistently, your health practices must evolve beyond convenience. They must become strategic.

Here are the four specific areas where I now invest every week with intention:

1. Preparation Over Willpower

People often rely on motivation to live healthily. I rely on planning. I schedule my meals in advance. I keep the right foods within reach. I choose hotels with gyms. I prepare for health in the same way I prepare for high-stakes business meetings because the ROI is higher.

2. Systematic Recovery

Most people think they're tired because they work hard. Often, they're tired because they never **fully** recover. I schedule recovery into my week. Short naps. Cold exposure. Walks without a phone. These aren't luxuries; they're productivity accelerators.

3. Functional Movement

I no longer train for vanity. I train for utility. My workouts are designed to strengthen posture, mobility, and stamina so I can perform at my peak on stage, in meetings, and under pressure. If it doesn't improve my function, it doesn't make the cut.

4. Environmental Support

Willpower is unreliable. So, I engineer my environment to make the right choices automatically. I keep filtered water within arm's reach. I use wearable sleep trackers. I batch healthy meals. The idea is simple: make success effortless by design.

The Truth About Alcohol and Performance

Let me be direct. **Alcohol compromises performance.**

Even moderate intake slows neural recovery, disrupts sleep architecture, dulls judgement, and weakens emotional control. For those in high-performance environments, it is a self-imposed disadvantage. There is nothing wrong with enjoying life, but when alcohol becomes routine, clarity becomes a casualty.

When I phased alcohol out of my life, it wasn't because of morality. It was because I recognised the cost. The difference in my cognition, my communication, and my decision-making was measurable.

You don't need to be extreme. But you must be honest. If something weakens your edge, question its place in your routine.

The Real Measure of Health

Here is the real question to ask yourself:

"Can I rely on my body when it matters most?"

When the presentation runs long. When sleep is short. When stress is high. When opportunity knocks and others hesitate, can you show up at your best?

If the answer is not a confident "yes," then your health is your next breakthrough.

You are not here to survive the day. You are here to drive it forward.

High energy is not a gift; it is a choice. It is a consequence of systems, discipline, and self-respect. You do not need to adopt a perfect routine. But you must build a reliable one. Because without sustained energy, the best version of you will remain a theory.

Action Steps: Building Strategic Health

1. Audit Your Energy Triggers

List five things that increase your energy and five that diminish it. Restructure your week to include more of the former and less of the latter.

2. Implement a 7-Day Reset

Remove one low-value habit for seven days: excess sugar, alcohol, or late-night screens. Monitor your focus and mood objectively.

3. Create a Recovery Ritual

Schedule two 30-minute sessions this week purely for recovery. No screens. No input. Just renewal. Build this into your calendar like any other high-value meeting.

4. Simplify Your Nutrition

Choose five core meals that support your performance and batch-prep them for the week. Eliminate decision fatigue around food.

5. Decide What Health Means to You

Write a one-sentence definition of health that aligns with your lifestyle and values. Let that sentence guide your next 90 days.

You do not need permission to be well. You only need discipline. Choose energy. Choose clarity. Choose the health that unlocks your potential.

CHAPTER 8: LEAD WITH POSITIVITY

The Eighth Rule of a 100X Life

The Discipline That Separates Leaders from Followers

One of the most misunderstood concepts in personal development is the idea of positivity.

Most people treat it as an emotion, something you either feel or don't feel, depending on the day. But those who lead with influence and build lasting success understand something far deeper:

In the same way you train your body, your mind must be conditioned. Because the truth is, your thoughts are not neutral, they are either constructing your future or sabotaging it. To think positively, especially when circumstances are difficult, is not naive. It is courageous. And it is necessary.

In my journey from a flat in Liverpool to building a global platform, I have seen optimism outperform intelligence, natural talent, and even experience. Time and time again, the individuals who rose highest were those who remained emotionally resilient in the face of uncertainty.

Why? Because positivity creates solutions. Negativity creates paralysis.

When you're leading a team, building a business, or navigating a personal storm, the one who can maintain composure and stay focused on progress will always become the centre of gravity. Others will follow their stability. Markets will respond to their clarity. Families will draw strength from their posture.

This is not emotional fluff. This is leadership psychology.

In crisis, pessimism is cheap. Anyone can panic. But positivity, grounded in discipline, informed by reality, and guided by purpose, is what separates real leaders from reactive individuals.

Positivity is not about blind hope. It is a trained neurological state. Numerous studies in neuroscience and behavioural psychology have shown that individuals who practise intentional gratitude, visualisation, and cognitive reframing have stronger immune responses, better decision-making, and greater resilience under stress.

Put simply, your mind adapts to what you feed it.

If you begin your day scanning for what is wrong, you will find more of it. If you begin your day scanning for progress, opportunities, and solutions, you will train your brain to operate at a higher level.

This is not wishful thinking. This is **mental conditioning**.

The highest performers are not always the most intelligent; they are the most emotionally trained.

Early in my career, I lacked emotional control. I would allow setbacks to affect my focus. A negative comment, a missed opportunity, or a delay would throw off my day, sometimes for hours. I assumed my mood was something I had to manage after it arrived.

I was wrong.

What I now know is this: **Emotions are not commands. They are signals. And signals can be re-routed.**

Here is the exact method I use to shift my emotional state on demand, especially when pressure rises:

1. Stop. Don't react.

Step back mentally. Take control of your breathing. Shift your physiology first.

2. Name it.

Identify what you're actually feeling. Is it anger? Frustration? Fear? The more specific, the more power you gain over it.

3. Reframe it.

Ask: *What else could this mean? What's good about this? What will I do with this energy?*

4. Direct it.

Decide on a new action, something immediate and forward-moving. Action interrupts negativity.

Over time, this process becomes automatic. You build emotional fluency. You respond instead of react. You operate with clarity even when pressure is high.

Choosing Light Over Darkness, Every Day

Life presents you with two choices every single day.

You can move towards the light, or you can sink into the dark.

Light means clarity, optimism, solutions, faith, and responsibility.

Darkness means confusion, blame, complaint, doubt, and resignation.

There is no neutral ground. Every thought you think, every word you speak, every decision you make is a vote towards one or the other.

I've known days when nothing went right, deals fell through, criticism flooded in, and personal challenges pressed heavily on my chest. But I also knew that how I responded in *those* moments would determine whether I remained stagnant or rose stronger.

And so, I chose light. Again. And again. And again.

That is not weakness. That's strength. That's leadership.

And that is the 100X mindset in action.

Positivity is not a perk of privilege. It is not a product of good weather, a winning streak, or easy circumstances. It is a practice. A decision. A leadership strategy.

It creates energy where others drain it. It opens doors where others see walls. And it brings out the best in you, even when you are still becoming your best self.

Action Steps: Leading With Positivity

1. Design a Daily Focus Question

Start each morning by asking: *"What's one thing I can do today to bring light into my environment?"* Act on it before noon.

2. Interrupt Negative Thought Loops

When you catch yourself spiralling mentally, stand up, take ten deep breaths, and redirect your attention to a solution-based question.

3. Build a Positivity Trigger

Identify one object (a bracelet, coin, or image) that reminds you to stay positive. Carry it with you and use it when stress rises.

4. Track Emotional Wins

Each evening, write down one situation where you chose optimism or resilience instead of frustration. This reinforces the habit.

5. Surround Yourself With Positive Voices

Curate your inputs. Listen to voices, read material, and connect with individuals who feed your faith, not your fear.

CHAPTER 9: ASK, BELIEVE, RECEIVE

The Ninth Rule of a 100X Life

Turning Vision into Measurable Outcomes

At some point in your journey, you must confront this truth: **What you expect from life shapes what life delivers to you.**

Not because of superstition. Not because of cosmic coincidence. But because, **your expectations direct your behaviour**, and your behaviour determines your outcomes.

Note that this has nothing to do with you believing in fairy tales, but rather, with your expectations that manipulate your behaviour.

This is the true foundation of the Law of Attraction. Not fantasy. Not wishful thinking. But disciplined mental alignment with a clearly defined outcome, followed by consistent, intelligent action.

Success, in every field, begins first in the mind.

Many people hear the phrase "ask, believe, receive" and mistake it for passive hope. They imagine that writing a goal in a journal or visualising wealth will automatically attract it. That is not how it works.

In truth, the Law of Attraction is simply the principle of **focused mental clarity** combined with **habitual action**.

You ask by setting a clear outcome. You believe by reinforcing that outcome through repetition and emotional commitment. You receive by aligning your decisions, standards, and efforts in a manner consistent with that outcome.

When these three are in harmony, results follow. When they are disconnected, effort is diluted.

Why Prayer, Belief and Repetition Matter

Whether you use the word "prayer," "intention," or "mental rehearsal," the concept is the same: you are training your mind to accept your goals as possible and to reject the noise of limitation.

Each morning, I speak my goals aloud, not to impress anyone, not to prove anything, but to programme myself to act in alignment. I visualise outcomes clearly. I state my targets confidently. I reinforce my standards daily.

Why? Because your subconscious does not follow instructions; it follows patterns. And patterns are built through repetition.

This is not spiritual theory. Your beliefs shape your perception. Your perception shapes your decisions. Your decisions shape your life.

If you want different results, change what you're rehearsing.

I remember when I began studying cryptocurrency, it wasn't popular. It wasn't mainstream. I had no roadmap, only conviction. I told myself, "There is a gap here, and I can fill it." That belief directed every action I took.

I began studying the market before sunrise. I built content. I created a brand. Not because it was easy but because I had already **seen it** in my mind.

Later, when I began building my audience, I had no budget for advertising. What I had was clarity of message, consistency of delivery, and a belief that what I was building would serve people. It did. Today, that platform reaches over a million.

I did not attract success by wishing. I attracted it by preparing and acting on what I saw before anyone else could see it. And that is what belief makes possible.

Here's where most people go wrong with vision: they make it emotional but not operational. A dream without structure is a distraction.

If you want to receive something from life, ask clearly. Write it down in measurable terms. Assign a deadline. Translate it into a system. Then believe, not by hoping, but by behaving as though it's already yours to earn.

This is how I create every breakthrough:

- First, I define the exact outcome.
- Then, I break it down into quarterly, monthly, and weekly actions.
- Then, I make those actions part of my daily identity.
- And finally, I measure progress without emotion. Numbers never lie.

Ask for what you want, not vaguely, but specifically. Believe in what you've asked for, not emotionally, but structurally. And receive, not by sitting back but by stepping up.

The Law of Attraction is not magic. It is mindset multiplied by movement. It is the alignment of belief and behaviour. When you combine those, life responds.

Action Steps: Applying Ask, Believe, Receive

1. Write One Clear Request

What do you truly want to create in the next 12 months? Write it in one sentence using the present tense. Be specific and measurable.

2. Create a Daily Mental Rehearsal

Spend five minutes visualising this outcome. See it. Hear it. Feel it. Embed it into your subconscious.

3. Break It Down

Convert the vision into strategic milestones. What must be done in the next 90 days, 30 days, and 7 days?

4. Link Belief to Behaviour

Identify one habit that aligns with this vision and commit to it daily. Belief must show up in action to produce results.

5. Track Emotional Drift

Note when doubt or discouragement appears. Record it. Reframe it. Replace it with deliberate action.

CHAPTER 10: BUILD WEALTH WITH PURPOSE

The Tenth Rule of a 100X Life

The Power of Money With Meaning

There comes a point in every journey where you realise that money, by itself, is not enough.

It will not satisfy you. It will not heal you. It will not define you.

But if you understand its true function **as a tool, as leverage, as a vehicle for purpose,** then wealth becomes not only possible but powerful. You begin building not just for income but for impact.

That is the kind of wealth worth pursuing. And it is the kind I chose to build.

Before I ever heard the word "crypto," I worked in finance. I studied the mechanics of the market, the flow of capital, and the emotional patterns behind investments. It was valuable and gave me my first insights into how money truly works.

But there was something missing: **ownership**.

I saw intelligent people earning high incomes but lacking control. Their time was bought. Their decisions were dictated. Their energy was absorbed by systems they didn't design. They were rich, but they were not free.

When I entered the crypto space in 2016, I brought with me a new question:

"What if I could build a financial platform that aligned with who I am and served others in the process?"

That shift from income-driven thinking to impact-aligned thinking was the beginning of true wealth.

Money, when earned ethically and invested intentionally, becomes a multiplier. It amplifies your values. It funds your mission. It supports your family. And it gives you the one resource most people never truly own: **choice**.

But this only happens when your income model matches your purpose.

Ask yourself: *Is the way I earn money aligned with what I believe in? With the kind of life I want to live? With the kind of contribution I want to make?*

If not, you're exchanging hours for validation, or worse, for survival.

In my case, building educational platforms, mentoring others, and helping people enter the decentralised economy gave me more than income. It gave me influence. And influence, when driven by integrity, outlasts currency.

Rich vs. Wealthy

Getting rich is a transaction. Building wealth is a transformation.

Being rich is temporary. It's a number. It comes and goes. Wealth is enduring. It is built on principles: discipline, generosity, patience, and strategic thinking.

Rich people buy more. Wealthy people **own more**: more time, more leverage, more assets, more peace.

I've been around both. I've seen the difference. One buys lifestyle, and the other builds a legacy.

Which one are you building?

If you grew up with financial scarcity, as I did, you likely absorbed limiting beliefs:

"Money is hard to make."

"Rich people are greedy."

"I'll never get ahead."

"I'm just not good with money."

These thoughts are not financial; they're emotional. And until they are addressed, no amount of earning will make you feel secure.

The turning point in my financial journey was not my first investment win. It was when I rewrote my internal script. I began telling myself:

"Money flows to value."

"My income grows as I grow."

"I am building something that lasts."

That mental shift changed my decisions, and my decisions changed my results.

If you want to grow financially, stop obsessing over tactics and start improving your mindset. Because **you will never outperform your self-image.**

And most people are under-earning because they are under-believing.

Wealth is not just about how much you earn. It's about how you earn it, why you earn it, and what it allows you to become in the process.

You are not here to chase income endlessly. You are here to build purpose through profit. To align your resources with your responsibility. To create freedom that you can share. Build your wealth with intention. Then, use it to build others.

Action Steps: Building Wealth With Purpose

1. Clarify Your Income Identity

Write down your current model for earning income. Then, write the kind of impact you want to have. Do they align? If not, revise your income strategy to reflect your values.

2. Define What Wealth Means to You

In one sentence, describe wealth, not in terms of money, but in terms of freedom, legacy, or contribution. Let that sentence guide your next financial decision.

3. Audit for Ownership

Review where you earn, save, and spend. Ask: *Am I building ownership or just paying obligations?* Adjust your strategy accordingly.

4. Challenge a Limiting Belief

Write down one money belief that has held you back. Replace it with a statement of empowerment. Say it aloud daily.

5. Build with the End in Mind

Choose one financial action this month that supports long-term wealth, starting an investment, launching a side income, or automating your savings. Act on it today.

CHAPTER 11: GIVE MORE THAN YOU TAKE

The Eleventh Rule of a 100X Life

Contribution as a Competitive Advantage

One of the great truths in wealth, leadership, and personal fulfilment is this:

You will be rewarded in direct proportion to the value you create for others.

This is not a philosophy. It is an economic law. And those who understand it early build careers, relationships, and legacies that compound over time because they are grounded in contribution.

In a world that often teaches people to ask, *"What can I get?"* those who lead with *"What can I give?"* always rise above the crowd.

When I first began to experience growth, financially and professionally, I made a critical observation: the more I gave, the more doors opened. The more I helped others solve real problems, the more leverage, trust, and income I attracted.

This was not about charity. It was about *alignment with value.*

The world compensates people who move it forward. That compensation may come in many forms: money, trust, access, opportunity, and influence. But the engine is always the same: **contribution.**

The most successful people I've met are those who understand this deeply. They operate with a giver's mindset, not because they expect something in return but because they understand how the value equation actually works.

They don't hoard ideas. They share insights.
They don't protect their time selfishly. They
invest it strategically.

They don't chase attention. They solve
problems. There is a simple equation I live by:

**You will be paid in proportion to the
problems you solve.**

If you solve small problems, you will receive
small rewards. If you solve complex, urgent,
and painful problems, you will be sought
after, remembered, and well-compensated.

This is how I built my reputation in the
crypto space. I didn't begin with millions. I
began with questions: *What are people confused
about? What are they afraid of? What are they
failing to understand?*

Then, I created resources, explained
concepts, and broke things down so others
could win. I wasn't just trading time for
income; I was becoming valuable.

And value is what makes you irreplaceable.
Being good at your craft is not enough.

In a world of automation, AI, and rapid commoditisation, **being good is expected.**

To truly stand out, you must be useful at a level that cannot be replicated easily. That happens through *service*.

Service is not about servitude. It's about foresight. It's the ability to anticipate what others need before they ask. It's the habit of doing more than required. It's the mindset that says, *"If I can help here, I will."*

This builds something rare: *trust*. And trust is the most valuable currency in the modern economy.

You become someone people turn to. Someone people rely on. Someone people promote when they're not in the room. That's how leaders are built. That's how legacies are formed.

Creating Win-Win Partnerships

One of the defining habits of high performers is their ability to think in win-win terms. They do not operate from scarcity.

They do not calculate every exchange. They ask: *"How can we both win here, long-term?"*

In my business dealings, whether with clients, investors, or partners, I learned that short-term wins at someone else's expense are always short-lived. But when I prioritised mutual benefit, deals moved faster. Trust deepened. Reputation grew. If you want to grow your influence, stop trying to outmanoeuvre people.

Start building partnerships that last longer than the contract.

Ask:

- *How can I make this person look good?*
- *How can I leave them better than I found them?*
- *What can I do that nobody else is willing to do here?*

That level of thinking creates loyalty. It builds your personal economy. And it elevates your identity far beyond your title or bank balance.

You are not paid for your presence. You are paid for your contribution.

Give more than you take, not to be liked, but to become valuable. Not to be praised but to become irreplaceable. In life, business, and relationships, the law remains constant: the more you give, the more you grow.

Action Steps: Giving With Strategy

1. Identify a Pain Point You Can Solve

In your work or community, find a problem that no one else is addressing well. Commit to solving it better than anyone.

2. Create a Value Habit

Choose one action each day where you add value without being asked. A solution. An insight. A connection. A thoughtful gesture.

3. Strengthen One Key Relationship

Reach out to someone you work with and ask, *"What can I do to support you better?"* Then, follow through without delay.

4. Offer More Than the Contract

In your next transaction or project, deliver one element that exceeds expectations. Build a reputation for generosity, not just competence.

5. Develop a Win-Win Filter

Before saying yes to any deal or partnership, ask: *"Is this sustainable for both parties?"* If not, redesign it.

CHAPTER 12: ELIMINATE WHAT HOLDS YOU BACK

The Twelfth Rule of a 100X Life

Success Requires Subtraction Before Expansion

There is a moment in every high-achiever's journey when they realise that success is not only about what you pursue; it's also about what you refuse to tolerate.

If you want to scale your life, your business, or your impact, you must develop the discipline to **cut away what no longer serves you.**

Not out of anger but out of alignment with who you are becoming.

Many people waste years trying to add more - more strategies, more goals, more tools - without ever examining what's draining them in the background.

But what you **remove** often matters more than what you pursue. It is the clutter, mental, emotional, and relational, that slows your momentum. It is the constant interruptions, toxic interactions, and low-return commitments that make success harder than it needs to be.

In my own life, I did not begin to accelerate until I began to **subtract**.

I stepped away from environments where I was tolerated, not challenged. I stopped engaging in conversations that led nowhere. I distanced myself from people who brought drama, not discipline.

This was not a moment of rebellion. It was a moment of realignment. And it changed everything.

Cutting Ties with What No Longer Aligns

Every person on the rise must make a critical decision:

Will I remain loyal to who I used to be, or will I become who I was meant to be?

That decision often involves **letting go** of:

1. People who consistently disrespect your time or vision
2. Habits that feel comfortable but lead nowhere
3. Digital distractions that fragment your attention
4. Obligations you said yes to out of guilt, not strategy

Elimination is not cruelty. It is clarity. It is the act of saying, *"This no longer fits the standard of the life I am building."*

You are not responsible for dragging everyone with you. You are responsible for protecting the energy that fuels your future.

Most people believe their breakthroughs will come from a new job, a new strategy, or a new opportunity. In reality, it comes from a new **internal standard**.

The most important environment you'll ever manage is your **inner environment**, the thoughts you entertain, the expectations you set, and the questions you ask yourself in silence.

If your inner world is reactive, scattered, or self-sabotaging, no amount of external success will bring peace. But if your inner world is focused, clear, and disciplined, success becomes a natural extension of who you are.

This is why I stopped managing time and started managing energy.

I eliminated inputs that caused decision fatigue.

I simplified my commitments.

I removed voices that created doubt.

Because when your mind is clean, your direction becomes clear.

You must decide what is acceptable and what is not. What earns your time and what no longer qualifies. What you will invest in and what you will leave behind.

When I made the decision to design my day with intention, I gained hours back. When I chose to engage only in conversations that build, not drain, I gained clarity. And when I let go of goals that were never mine to begin with, I gained direction.

A high-standard life is not a busy life. It is a focused life. It is simple but not small. It is intense but not chaotic. It is strategic, not reactive. This is the life the 100X Mindset demands.

You do not rise by adding more noise. You rise by removing what no longer belongs.

Progress is not about doing everything. It is about doing the **right things** and having the courage to eliminate the rest.

Your next breakthrough may not require something new. It may require you to walk away from what is no longer worthy of you.

Action Steps: Strategic Elimination

1. Audit Your Energy Leaks

Write down three things, people, or habits that consistently drain your energy. Choose one to eliminate this week.

2. Set a New Standard

In one sentence, define what is now non-negotiable in your life, whether it be time, boundaries, conversations, or habits.

3. Schedule a Subtraction Day

Block two hours this week to review your calendar, commitments, and environment. Eliminate or delegate everything that doesn't align with your core vision.

4. Conduct a Relationship Check-In

Ask: *Who adds energy to my life? Who diminishes it?* Begin spending more time with the former and phasing out the latter.

5. Create a Decision Filter

Before saying yes to anything, ask: *Does this move me closer to the life I'm designing?* If not, decline with confidence.

CHAPTER 13: LIVE WITH A WARRIOR SPIRIT

The Thirteenth Rule of a 100X Life

Resilience Is a Skill, Not a Gift

There is a harsh but liberating truth you must embrace if you wish to live an extraordinary life:

Life is not meant to be easy.

It is meant to forge you.

There will be setbacks you did not expect. Losses you cannot explain. Delays you did not deserve. If you are not prepared to meet resistance, you are not prepared to lead.

But here's the truth I've built my life upon:

Life is hard. But you are harder.

This is the mindset of a warrior. Not in armour, but in attitude. Not in rage but in resilience.

You do not need to shout to be powerful. But you must decide: *Nothing will break me.*

The Season That Tested Everything

There was a time in my life when I had nothing but a vision and not much else.

No security.

No savings.

No applause.

No one coming to rescue me.

Rent overdue. Phone disconnected. Rejections mounting. And still, I woke up, showed up, and refused to surrender. Why? Because somewhere deep inside me, I had already chosen: *I will outlast this.*

Resilience is not loud. It's not glamorous. It's getting up when no one is watching. It's doing what's required, without excuses, without complaint, without shortcuts.

That season did not ruin me. It revealed me.

The most valuable skill in today's world is not intelligence or talent.

It's **emotional stamina**, the ability to remain composed, decisive, and forward-moving while others break down.

The modern world rewards those who keep going.

This is not about ignoring the pain. It's about learning how to process it without being paralysed by it.

That's what grit is. Grit is not pretending everything's fine.

Grit is doing what must be done, especially when it's not fine.

Most people fold too early. They take a single loss as a sign they should stop. But high performers understand something different:

Setbacks are feedback. Not finish lines.

If you feel tired, rest, don't quit.

If you feel overwhelmed, breathe, don't retreat. You are not weak for feeling pressure. You are only weak if you allow it to influence your decisions.

Being unbreakable is not a personality trait. It is a daily practice.

Here are three principles I use to keep my mind strong when the pressure builds:

1. Control the narrative.

I do not allow fear to finish my thoughts. I interrupt doubt with discipline. I replace *"What if I fail?"* with *"What must I learn?"*

2. Find the opportunity inside the adversity.

Every situation contains an advantage for the one who remains calm enough to see it. My greatest business ideas came during personal setbacks.

3. Never let emotion dictate your identity.

You may feel discouraged. You may feel alone. But you are still the same person who made the decision to grow. Anchor to that version, not your lowest moment.

This is how warriors are built, not by avoiding chaos but by becoming calm within it.

You Are Not Here to Be Fragile

You were not designed to crumble under pressure.

You were made to rise through it.

Too many people are taught to avoid discomfort. To stay in their lane. To numb the pain. But warriors understand: **Discomfort is where the work is.**

In discomfort, you expand.

In adversity, you adapt.

In pressure, you evolve.

This is the spirit I carry into every negotiation, every challenge, every season of uncertainty.

It is the same spirit that brought me from a council flat in Liverpool to global influence.

Not because I had all the answers. But because I made one decision, again and again:

I will not break. I will build.

You will not win every battle. But you must refuse to lose the war.

Strength is not born in success. It is built-in resistance.

And if you are willing to fight forward when others shrink back, you will build a life few ever taste, not because it was easy, but because you refused to collapse.

Action Steps: Build a Warrior Spirit

1. Define Your Core Fight

Write down one challenge you're facing right now. Then, write a sentence that declares your response, not your fear, but your *fight*.

2. Anchor a Resilience Routine

Choose one action you'll do daily, no matter what, be it training, writing, meditating, or cold exposure. This builds mental certainty.

3. Track Your Recovery Time

When setbacks happen, write down how long it takes you to refocus. Aim to shrink that time. The shorter the gap, the stronger your resilience.

4. Build Your Warrior Mantra

Craft a one-line statement that represents your resolve. For example: *"I do not quit. I recalibrate."* Repeat it when pressure rises.

5. Keep One Promise to Yourself This Week

Honour one commitment that stretches you. Not because it's convenient but because your character depends on it.

The world doesn't need more comfort. It needs more warriors.

Stand your ground. Stay your course. And let your life prove your strength.

CHAPTER 14: LEAD THE LIFE FEW DARE TO IMAGINE

The Fourteenth Rule of a 100X Life

The Life You Want Exists on the Other Side of Who You're Willing to Become

And as a final rule, I want you to think about this: Most people don't fail because they lack the ability.

They fail because they lack the **audacity**.

The audacity to think beyond survival. The audacity to define success for themselves.

The audacity to live on their terms, with their standards, regardless of what others expect.

But here is the truth I discovered, first on a cold morning in Liverpool, then on stages, inside markets, and across countries:

You are only ever one decision away from an entirely different life.

Not a small upgrade. Not a minor improvement. But a total transformation if you are willing to lead yourself into the unknown.

This is the difference between the many who wish... and the few who lead.

What It Means to Lead Your Life

Leadership is not about position. It's about ownership. To lead your life means you stop waiting for conditions to be right. You stop blaming the past. You stop waiting for validation.

You take the pen. You write the story. You accept the consequences of bold decisions.

I've met thousands of people who say they want to live differently, more freely, more purposefully, more abundantly. But when it comes to execution, they wait.

1. They wait for the economy to shift.
2. They wait for support from people who've never led anything.
3. They wait for permission from systems that never intended for them to win.

If that is you, hear me clearly: **No one is coming to rescue you.** And that is not a tragedy. It's a turning point.

You were born to lead your life, not lease it out.

There is a version of life that the world hands to you by default.

Study hard. Get a safe job. Make an acceptable income. Keep your head down. Don't question the rules. Retire quietly.

There is nothing wrong with that unless your heart is asking for more. And if you're reading this, it is.

To lead a life only a few dare to imagine means:

- You set goals that scare you but build you.
- You create value at levels others haven't even considered.
- You invest in discipline when others chase distraction.
- You keep rising long after comfort would have told you to stop.

It's not always glamorous. It's not always applauded. But it is always worth it. Because one day, the life you once imagined becomes the life you now live. And that is what legacy is built on.

Vision Must Be Matched With Execution

If you want to lead a bold life, you must build systems that support bold living.

It's not enough to journal dreams or attend motivational events. You must turn your decisions into discipline. You must turn your ambition into execution.

Ask yourself:

- *What structures support the person I'm becoming?*
- *What actions would the future version of me take today?*
- *What would I pursue if I didn't need applause, only alignment?*

The most powerful leaders I know don't just dream.

1. They act.
2. They track.
3. They review.
4. They adapt.
5. And they **never forget who they're doing it for.**

You don't need to wait for a title to be a leader. You don't need to wait for perfection to begin.

You lead every time you act with integrity. You lead every time you keep a promise to yourself.

You lead every time you raise the standard instead of lowering the goal.

I didn't become Mando CT because someone gave me a plan. I became who I am because I stopped negotiating with mediocrity. I decided that my children, my audience, my future, and my creator deserved the strongest, most intentional version of me.

That decision belongs to you now.

A 100X life is not about doing more.

It is about becoming more strategic, consistent, and unapologetic.

Most will not choose this. Most will settle. But you are not most.

You are here to lead. To build. To elevate. And to live a life that, years from now, others point to and say, *"That's what's possible."*

Action Steps: Lead Your Life

1. Write Your Legacy Sentence

In one line, describe the kind of life you want to be remembered for. Make it clear. Make it strong.

2. Establish a Quarterly Leadership Goal

Choose one outcome you will own over the next 90 days. Break it into 12 weekly actions. Execute relentlessly.

3. Build a Decision Filter

Ask: *Does this align with the future I've chosen?* If not, walk away. Every decision is either building your future or costing it.

4. Reinforce Identity Daily

Each morning, declare who you are becoming and act accordingly. Identity shapes action. Action shapes destiny.

5. Expand Your Environment

Spend time with people who expect excellence. Who live boldly. Who have

already done what you once thought
impossible.

Don't just imagine a great life. **Lead it.** The
world follows those who lead themselves
first.

CONCLUSION: YOUR 100X LIFE STARTS TODAY

The Future You Want Is Waiting for the Present You to Commit

There is no secret. There is only a standard. And the moment you decide to meet it, your life begins to change.

If you've read this book carefully, you'll notice something: I haven't asked you to wish harder. I've challenged you to *build* better. Not just once, but daily.

Because success is not an event; it is a system. A system built on clarity, energy, integrity, contribution, resilience, and execution, repeated **with precision and intent.**

This is how every transformation occurs. Not by hoping. By **deciding**.

There is always one moment that separates the past from the future. One decision that draws the line in the sand. One internal command that says:

"From today, I operate differently."

This doesn't require perfect conditions. It doesn't require applause. It requires one thing only: **alignment between who you say you are and what you repeatedly do.**

Your environment won't change until your expectations do. Your bank account won't change until your identity does. Your outcomes won't change until your standards rise.

But once they do, everything moves with them.

You are not here by accident. And the results you've been attracting are not random; they are reflections of your focus, discipline, and consistency.

The universe is not withholding from you. It's waiting for you to show up in alignment, with clarity, with responsibility, and with daily proof that you are serious.

You do not attract what you want. You attract what you demonstrate readiness for.

That readiness is built into your habits.
And habits are shaped by systems.
This book has been your framework.
However, the framework is useless without **implementation**.

So, I leave you with this challenge, not for inspiration, but for identity:

The 90-Day Challenge: Become Unrecognisable

For the next 90 days:

1. Live by your highest standard, not your mood.

2. Execute the 100X habits with no negotiation.

3. Track your progress. Refuse excuses. Own every outcome.

4. Eliminate distractions that dilute your direction.

5. Lead your life with the same precision you'd expect from the world's top performer because that's who you're becoming.

Do this, and you won't just make progress. You will become **unrecognisable** to those who knew the old you and even to the version of you reading this now.

THE FINAL WORD

You are no longer waiting for a breakthrough. You are the breakthrough. You've read enough books. You've made enough notes. Now it's time to move. Not someday. **Today.**

The 100X Life isn't out there somewhere.

It starts here.

It starts now.

It starts with you.

To your success,

If you're ready to turn this knowledge into a personal transformation, join the global 100X movement. You'll gain access to exclusive resources, challenges, mentorship updates, and tools to help you implement the 100X lifestyle with precision.

Start now at:

☞ www.100x-mindset.com

ABOUT THE AUTHOR

Mando CT is a global entrepreneur, crypto leader, and creator of *The 100X Mindset*. From humble beginnings in Liverpool to financial freedom in Dubai, his journey spans investment banking, digital assets, and personal transformation. Through discipline, resilience, and belief, he built a life few dare to imagine. Today, he mentors others to do the same—turning mindset into mastery.

Learn more at: www.100x-mindset.com